IN SWEET HARMONY

poetry *pt* today

IN SWEET HARMONY

Edited by Suzy Walton

First published in Great Britain in 2001 by Poetry
Today, an imprint of
Penhaligon Page Ltd, Remus House, Coltsfoot Drive,
Woodston, Peterborough. PE2 9JX

© Copyright Contributors 2001

All rights reserved. No part of this publication may be
reproduced, stored in a retrieval system, or transmitted
in any form or by any means, without prior permission
from the author(s).

A Catalogue record for this book is available from the
British Library

ISBN 1 86226 617 4

Typesetting and layout, Penhaligon Page Ltd, England.
Printed and bound by Forward Press Ltd, England

Foreword

In Sweet Harmony is a compilation of poetry, featuring some of our finest poets. This book gives an insight into the essence of modern living and deals with the reality of life today. We think we have created an anthology with a universal appeal.

There are many technical aspects to the writing of poetry and *In Sweet Harmony* contains free verse and examples of more structured work from a wealth of talented poets.

Poetry is a coat of many colours. Today's poets write in a limitless array of styles: traditional rhyming poetry is as alive and kicking today as modern free verse. Language ranges from easily accessible to intricate and elusive.

Poems have a lot to offer in our fast-paced 'instant' world. Reading poems gives us an opportunity to sit back and explore ourselves and the world around us.

Contents

My Broken Old Car	Fay Jacqueline Gardener	1
The Progression Of Life	James Coatsworth	2
Observances	Belle Wood	4
The Joys Of Motherhood?	Annette Carswell	5
Dance To The Music Of Time	Kath Gabbitas	6
Healing Prayer	Liz Gibbs	7
After The Flood	Wendy Searle	8
Missing You	Jill Tester	9
A Flower	Magdalene Chadwick	10
Triton Among The Minnows	Gemma Green	11
No Flowers	N Harvey	12
Parting	Jill Green	13
Sentiments Of Christmas	Julie A Smith	14
The Shell	Sandie Keggans	16
Millennium Window	Audrey Wilson	17
Elsa	Carole Pratt	18
Drinker's Lament	Linda Duff	20
Chechnya	Amii Nettleingham	21
The Museum	Sarah Knapton	22
Howden Moor	A C Alderson	23
Believe	Nichola Brown	24
Conversation	Alison Rutherford	25
Innocence Lost	Carole Davis	26
Fly Away Home	Claire Frances Simpson	27
Gone	Diana M Annely	28
Untitled	A Taylor	29
Without You	Susan Mason	30
The Earth	Lisa Helen Venus	31
Untitled	Evelyn/Amy McFadzean	32
With Her	Edward B Evans	33
Goodnight My Someone	Jonathan P Heath	34
The Divide	Lorna Marlow	35
Weightcare ~		
Slimmer Of The Year	E A Barber	36
That Winter's Night	E M Brooks	38
The Rose	Samuel Gordon Ainsley	39

I Sit By My Window	Maurice Bailey	40
Choice	Corwin V Barber	41
My World	Ryan Smith	42
The Wasp	Scott Smith	43
Painting A Picture Of October	Janet Marie James	44
In This Life	Paul Esser	45
The Horrid Potion	Owen Fleming	46
Love	Seema Gill	47
Mother	John Flanagan	48
My Old Town	John Birch	49
The Tree Of Life	Joyce Metcalfe	50
Contentment	Eleanor M Parker	51
Black Mountain And Its Valleys	Sylvia Farr	52
Greed	Edna Bainbridge	53
The Apple Tree	Mary D Woodman	54
A Husband's Lament	R M Dodds	55
Devon Sunset	Iris Reeves Williams	56
Heroes	James Kinsey	57
Winter	Val Nichols	58
Sorrow	Rosalie McDuffus	59
Time To Stop	Victor James Gunstone	60
Idyll	Dennis A Brunning	61
Holiday In Pembrokeshire	Denis Parry	62
Dragon's Breath	J Annetts	63
Moon Thoughts	J Robertson	64
My Wandering Spirit	Rosemarie Bruce	65
A Gosling's Breast	C A Brown	66
Autumn	Jade Murphy Symonds	67
Angels	Patricia Brett	68
No News	Carole E Drew	69
Aurora	Martin J MacInnes	70
Helping Hand	Mary Whittaker	72
Anglesey	Alan Hougardy	73
Dreams	Iris E Weller	74
A Blanket Of Darkness	Maura Rea	75
Beyond Love	M Belton	76
The Rose	Jennifer Ferguson	78
Untitled	Lyn Spencer	79

The Mighty Power	Kerry Byng	80
Have You Ever?	Michelle Gray	81
Memories	Mary Singleton McLelland	82
Nature	Jamie Lawrence Curtis	84
Sun	Thomas William Cameron	85
Nobody In Particular	Lauri Love	86
New Year's Eve 2000	Kate Woodruff	87
Prancer	Jose Evelyn	88
A Dignified Silence	Phil Jones	89
The Friesan	Jill Wilmore	90
War Of Freedom	Linda Wright	91
Church	NJM	92
The Game	Rob Mears	93
Never-Ending Love	Charles Hepburn	94
Skywalking	Wendy Grant	95
The Man	Stevie	96
Touch Not My Soul	Valerie Atkins	97
A Complex Woman	Heather M Marsland	98
Dreams	Diana Price	99
In Memory	E M Evans	100
In The Millennium	Sammi Walsh	102
Mother	Helen McGregor	103
To My Valentine	Sue Southgate	104
Washing Day	Shirley Boyce	106
Youth	Phyllis Stark	107
Just Twenty-Four Hours	M Cadman	108
An Invitation	Cath Little	109
Grandad	John Leslie Pearson	110
Sunshine	Kirsten Somerville	111
Tell Me	Paula O'Hare	112
This England	Dave Gammon	113

My Broken Old Car

I knew when I parked the car last night
That I'd have trouble in the morning.
With hesitation I sat in and turned the key,
If cars have a throat, mine's got a bad cough!
Coughing and choking, choking and spluttering!
As it winced, the car slowly wheezed . . .
And then dried with a judder.
The turn of the key brought silence.
It was time to walk.

Fay Jacqueline Gardner (12)

The Progression Of Life

Wastage is from uncertainty
Uncertainty a waste of time
Time is a rare virtue
A virtue is a rhyme

A rhyme is an expression
An expression on the face
Faces all around us
Around us only haste

Haste is people rushing
People rushing for their jobs
Jobs keep us going
Going to the dogs

Dogs are on all fours
Four sides are what surround
Surrounded by the sky above
The sky above the ground

The ground is the bottom
The bottom is the last
Last is the loser
A loser has no past

The past is things remembered
Remembered then forgot
Forgotten and abandoned
Abandon the entire lot

Lots of space available
Availability's a sin
Sins aren't always deadly
Deadly from within

Within is not the outside
Outside of what is me
Me is an object of wastage
Wastage is from uncertainty

James Coatsworth

Observances

Does nature strike alone the fancy of the poet?
Can the seething mass of men stare, dumb, then turn
blind eyes, unaffected, unaware, from sights
which stun the mind and cause the eyes to burn?
For I have stood in the shadows cast
by heaven-brushing pines and giant firs
while yonder Apollo breathed his last
but with one radiant arrow defied the dark.
I have walked on snowy, sunlit afternoons
and heard the untimely singing of the lark,
while ten million rosened crystals sparkled on the hill,
as twilight set the snow to rosy fire,
and the lake shone in its glassy chill.
From dizzying heights I've watched green fields below
like some ever-changing verdant patchwork quilt,
turn yellow with the mustard, or violet where the bluebells grow.
Is this love of nature but a learnéd art?
Can we alone of all the species love
these sights ~ are we of all the creatures set apart?
For these visions, when with our faculties are met
quicken the soul within the sapient man;
and though we are still lowly, we may be as gods yet.

Belle Wood

The Joys Of Motherhood?

'Of course I'm not alright, you fool!
    Stop mopping my head. Go sit on that stool.
Give me the gas, give something I beg,
    A shot of Pethadine ~ here in my leg.
Please knock me out, I've had enough.
    Nobody warned me it would be this tough!
I'm going to push whatever you say,
    I want this over without delay!
What do you mean: 'Just wait and pant?'
    Superwoman is something I ain't!
Several hours of endless pain ~
    I'm *never* going through this again!
Thank heaven's it's over ~ I'm shattered,
    They say he's alright, that's all that mattered.

Ten little fingers and ten little toes,
    And just look at his gorgeous wee nose!
So many flowers, and cards, and gifts,
    All the pain, the tears and anguish just lifts.
Seeing our wee miracle in his hospital cot,
    Could I really have meant that he'd be our lot?!

Annette Carswell

Dance To The Music Of Time

It only seems like yesterday
since you held my hand in yours
on that cold and windy day in
May or was it June and said you
would never leave me on my own

Now as I sit here by your side
and hold your hand in mine
the memories of so long ago
come flooding back

We walked down the aisle
arm in arm and made a promise
until death do us part then
war came and tore us apart
but you promised you would be back

For sixty years we danced
to the music of time
now the music has stopped
and time has run out
and this time you will
not be coming back

I let go of your hand
for the last time and
close my eyes and
we dance to
the music of time

Kath Gabbitas

Healing Prayer

Trying gently
  to explain
    without wanting to hurt.

Still the pain
  on recall.
Crying, hurting
  not understanding
    reasoning
      explaining.
A little deeper now the realisation
  maybe anger
    yet understanding
      then love
      real love.

The truth,
  always the truth
  sets you free.
Unlock your soul.
  Let yourself be
    healed.

Liz Gibbs

After The Flood

Left unwanted by the side of the road,
Sometimes alone, sometimes with others,
Wet, squashed, guts spilling out,
Feet pass by but nobody bothers.
I was needed once, not long ago,
They couldn't get enough.
Now discarded no-one cares
And life is pretty tough.
You may wonder what I am?
Left to rot like a piece of rag,
They'll need me again before very long,
Say 'chuck us another sand bag'.

Wendy Searle

Missing You

Oh mother dear I feel you near
Why it's so strange 'cos you're not here
I see your pictures all around
I hear your voice, but hear no sound
I feel the love that once surrounded me
I long to feel your arms around me
Oh give me strength to bear the pain
Of never seeing your dear face again
And yet I know that one fine day
I'll see your face
But that will be in a far better place
But now I grieve for the greatest loss
And I know I must bear this cross
Until the day, I know not when
When we shall once more meet again

Jill Tester

A Flower

A flower is so tender
And yet so strong,
Like a small bird at dawn
Who renders his beautiful song.
A feather is so light
When it floats on high,
Like a soapy rainbow bubble,
Rising up to the sky.
I like blowing bubbles
And watching them rise,
But all too soon they drift away
Still, tomorrow is another day.

Magdalene Chadwick

Triton among the Minnows

Grandad stoops with the countenance of a bowler
letting the water sneak over
the lip of our margarine tub.

The sky turns. Swatches of orange and dry bird song
His hand, measured as a seamstress
swoops to the belly of the stream.

He emerges, wet past his shirt sleeves
Pelican in victory
tiny fish flutter under old oak eyes.

We head home. Riding high on his shoulders
I smell the night cool in his hair.
Behind us, a single set of prints, already shrinking.

Gemma Green

No Flowers

The only tiger, you kissed the lazy summer,
The meadow's wind.
The general running across history,
Stood by the gate torch in hand
Groping the cannon's fodder,
Honour grows faint alone,
Youth is born in that gown.
Smoke and cinder, enamel doors shine.
And salty nature kissed me.
Purity before its time
Retirement too old.

N Harvey

Parting

Such tenuous threads to Earth we hold,
And of these threads Love is the Gold.
A thread that stretches while we're apart,
Yet keeps us close to each other's heart.
Love holds memories of times gone by,
Happy, sad, sometimes a sigh,
Love is healing, reaching to you,
And wherever you are
My love is with you.
Your future is bright, with love all around,
Your spirit is strong ~ nothing will confound.
The days of sunshine yet to be,
Enjoy them all and live ~ for me.

Jill Green

Sentiments Of Christmas

Twinkling lights dress the windows
Where a host of noses have been pressed
Looking at delights inside
Deciding which toy is best

An old chap selling chestnuts
Like as in the days of old
Huddled round the glowing embers
To keep out the biting cold

A group of children sweetly singing
Whilst shoppers gather round
A respite from the shopping rush
A moment's peace is found

Turkeys hanging from the butcher's window
To tempt the passer-by
With holly wreaths and mistletoe
That catch the straying eye

Queues for Father Christmas
As excited children wait
Mothers, smiling, hold their hands
And hope he won't be late

A church full of candles, light and hope
A host of angels sing
Others sit beside the fire
Wondering what Christmas Day will bring

Christmas morning, music playing
Cracking nuts and drinking wine
Turkey spitting in the oven
And merriment sublime

Young or old, rich or poor
The Christmas message's clear
The peacefulness it brings about
Gives us hope for another year.

Julie A Smith

The Shell

On the sand I see a pine-cone made of shell.
I pick it up. It is hazy brown in colour
with a solid white band wrapped once around it.
I note the base, a pin-hole in the centre
with a light brown line spiralling out from it.
As I hold it to my cheek I feel its smoothness,
like that of a stone in a riverbed.
When I put it to my ear it is the echo of the sea
yet in the palm of my hand it is cool and solid.
It appears wrapped like an autumn leaf
with a rough, uneven edge concealing what is inside.
As I peer closely at it, the white powdery inside
looks like the surface of the moon
with its round indentations and coarse heights.
A curious scent leaks from inside the concave casing
and clings to my throat. It reminds me of lemon sherbet.

Sandie Keggans

Millennium Window

Horizon of millennium
Dawn of Expectation
Unknown potential concealed
In its mysterious depths.

Generations of mankind
Hesitate at the entrance
To the vortex of the future
Where unexplained dangers await.

Visionary Sages predict
Celestial upheaval
Relentless waves of adversity
Mists of despair.

Window of the millennium
Opportunity of our planet
Emerging out of darkness
Into an expectant future.

Audrey Wilson

Elsa

'Elsa' was not my dog
~ but I loved her just the same,
I met her owner through her ~
David, was his name.

He used to bring her to the park,
Along with 'Simba' too,
~ and I'd watch them all play awhile,
'Til slowly, my love grew.

'Elsa' began to greet me,
~ running forward ~ tail held high,
A Great Dane, like a Lioness
But with such a gentle, kindly eye.

She'd leave her hairs all over me
And slobber on my clothes ~
But such was my devotion,
I'd just smile and kiss her nose.

'Simba' ~ an affectionate Dobermann,
~ I grew fond of him as well,
But what the future held for us,
No-one then, could tell . . .

Something strange tho' happened
Sometime in the Fall ~
I missed them all so greatly,
~ they didn't come at all . . .

Those Winter days were lonely,
Then Spring was on the way,
The days were getting lighter,
~ and they came back to me one day.

Along with Summer sunshine
~ the bond between us grew,
Good times, like these, don't last
~ somehow, I just knew . . .

Summer turned once more to Winter ~
'Til that fateful Christmas Day,
She took ill quite suddenly
And next day ~ she passed away.

'Elsa' ~ how we all shall miss you,
You will never know ~
Not just your grieving owner,
~ I too, will miss you so . . .

And now that you have left us ~
This ache inside me burns
For I know, this time ~ you won't come back,
When the Spring returns . . .

Carole Pratt

Drinker's Lament

(Dedicated to my mother, Wilma Duff,
who passed away on 27th February 2000)

I emptied the glass time and again
I always had my fill
And now I lie beneath the ground
Silent, cold and still

One more drink to calm the nerves
One more drink to cope
I couldn't have done it better
If I'd been given a hanging rope

I'd say I'm sorry but it's too late
To those I've left behind
I couldn't see what harm I'd done
The booze, it numbs the mind

Too late for me, but not for you
So heed this fateful warning
Think before you drink tonight
And live to see the morning

Linda Duff

Chechnya

A cold winter's day, a shadowy night,
We maintain our freedom, that's how it will stay,
There are times of emotion, but life is all right,
We can be ourselves, that's life's usual way.

Where cold Russian hearts, bring shadowy smiles,
These times have began and then they have passed,
Where hardship and pain's not unknown for miles,
The thought's later sadly erased from our hearts.

A soldier stands, with a look of detest,
With an AK47 in the crook of his arm.
He is attired in olive, alike to the rest,
Disguising his hatred to save him from harm.

A Chechen looks up; he is fighting his tears,
Holds his palms to the sky, as the stars they collide.
He turns to his wife; they've been hiding for years,
But alas they are found, all to do is abide.

A child and its mother, walk on with no shoes,
To save the whole family, themselves, to elude.
But the borders known joy, brings tragedy's news,
The home they adored will an army intrude.

Like the hopes they destroyed they will conquer the doors,
Torture the people, the ones that remained.
Set up a system, to agree to their laws,
Or to torture and sadden for punishment's pain.

A shadowy night, a cold winter's day,
A gun and a soldier, whom of his life has hate.
A child and a mother alone all the way,
The country for peace is determined to wait.

Amii Nettleingham

The Museum

We dodged the bullets, found a place to bide
Our time in the doorway then we stepped inside,
Through debris, dust and mingled lives
A place for pretty things to hide.
We advanced, afraid, on the preserved past,
Carefully captured behind yellowing glass.
The present forgotten, history amassed,
Now forgotten again in a future bypassed.

We walked along the vacant aisles,
Mocked by masks from tattered tiles,
And through the portrait perfect smiles
Death looked on with weary eyes,
With Wanderlust we trekked this tomb,
Embraced within nostalgia's womb
When stumbling through the gathered gloom
We brought to light the secret room.

Sarah Knapton

Howden Moor

Grey clouds sullenly brood on the horizon
The undulating masses of the moors rise dauntingly.
Sour land, tufted with stippled grasses.
Black peat drinks the moisture of ages,
And pours its excesses in narrow gullies, lined with
fossils and the skulls of sheep.
Draining to the thread of grey tarmac, which toils its
way across the land, and here pools, in stagnant
slime, as if in disgust at human intrusion.
Ravaged by the elements
It yields in bitter fertility.
Its creations wild and harsh.
Iron grasses, each strand wind whipped and rain
raked to a raw red blade.
Bushes and Flora, stunted travesties of their kind.
The devil-eyed sheep, are born, and die in this
pitiless dampness.
And only the plover sobs,
On the morning air.

A C Alderson

Believe

Is it a fight to find what we are looking for?
True happiness, faith and dreams galore.
For me my life has been not a bore,
Instead a challenge, determined not to flaw.

For what is it that we fear?
Not to have made our mark, our name unheard of in our atmosphere.
We should all concentrate on our own true beliefs,
Our inner soul, the intuition, what makes us sleep.

Wake up tomorrow and truly believe,
You can do anything you please.
Fulfil that dream you had last night,
Just believe . . .

I can see why people fail at what they do,
They've had their confidence destroyed
And as a result feel a fool too.
Ignore the failures of others around you,
Instead concentrate on your goals,
Your life ahead of you.

Rejoice your life for it is very short,
A book it may be because it has a beginning and an end,
But no chapters will evolve unless you find,
True love and happiness that lay before mankind.

Nichola Brown

Conversation

She often talks to him, passing a remark here and there,
needing reassurance that the vegetables are not overcooked
or sharing a flash of annoyance at a pile of junk-mail,
an empty milk-carton which should have been enough till tomorrow,
rain, when sunshine had been promised.

She doesn't expect a response, so that when it does come
in the stirring outside her window of the elm tree,
in the faint sound of soot falling behind the gas fire
or the cool silence of a day too soon woken into,

the room will hold still for a moment
and she will pause, remembering.

Alison Rutherford

Innocence Lost
(A child's prayer)

Little Jesus in the sky
Take me to be with you up high
Amongst the bright and twinkling stars
Up with Jupiter and Mars

I don't want to be in my little bed
I'd rather be with you instead
For this bed is a place of shame
Of things so bad I cannot name

Take me from my night of sorrow
Till fresh clean sun brings new tomorrow
Keep me safe from the fear and dread
Which makes me wish that I was dead

The dark secrets I've locked up inside
Are of adults' sins I've learned to hide
But years of sadness and the tears
Have made me old beyond my years

Little Jesus do you see
Children of abuse the same as me
I sometimes wonder if you know
This hell where youth and innocence go?

Carole Davis

Fly Away Home

Fly little young one
I wish I could come
Spread out your wings and just fly like your chums
With your pale Bashe eyes
You're sure to do well
A couple of days and I'm sure you'll recover well
Bounce up with your chest with its fiery red colours
And let your wings just spring to life
Get rid of all your strife
And fly away home

Claire Frances Simpson

Gone

Still I stand, I stare, I wait,
I think, I dream, I ponderously anticipate,
I do not feel happiness, I do not feel pain,
I do not think I will feel again.

But surely there should be something
Just even an emptiness there,
Something to show that you came,
Something to show, that you cared.

Take all, take all, take all you must
That's beautiful away,
But please at least return to me,
What used to be, my heart.

Diana M Annely

Untitled

Your kisses brush over my skin
Like autumn leaves falling and
Caressing the terracotta earth.
They sparkle like stardust, tripping,
Wheeling, diving ~ spreading silver
Shards of light icicles that
Burn into my mind.

A Taylor

Without You

Let the last clock tick
To leave not a sound
Let the leaves blow in the breeze
To fall forlornly to the ground

I do not want to hear
The chorus of birds
Chirping in the morning
They witness the dawning
Of another dragging day

Gazing out of my window
The world seems almost still
Calm and tranquil
I sit there watching wistfully
A feeling of melancholy
I wonder if you are thinking of me
Wherever you are
I hope it is not that far

Switch off the sun
To leave night instead of day
Unplug the rivers, lakes and oceans
Let planet Earth decay
We are all dying anyway

Nobody beckons death to come
Yet it comes much too early for some
It came in the blink of an eye for you
Ever since
I wait patiently
For death to come to me too
There is nothing here
Without you

Susan Mason

The Earth

Every day holds something new, now I can do so many things,
I'm ready for the day ahead prepared for what it brings:

I'd love to go and change the world,
don't cut down all our trees
We need what God above provides,
so don't pollute our seas

Don't test on little animals,
they really need our care
To hurt and kill for our own use,
just simply isn't fair

The starving living far away,
need food like you and I
If they had more to eat and drink
a few less then would die

The ozone too is breaking up,
the sun dries up the land
Flowers, fruit and vegetables
just give the world a hand

The earth is dying more each day
be at peace and do not fight
As long as I am in this world
I'll try and make it right!

Lisa Helen Venus

Untitled

I have a dream of how the world should be,
No more famine, war or poverty,
Lots of sunshine, a little rain,
No more earthquakes, floods or hurricanes.

There's no more poor, we'd all be rich,
No more diseases, no more sick,
Plenty to eat and plenty to drink,
And we'd all live in houses all coloured pink.

Lots of happiness, no more sorrow,
Let's all be friends, starting from tomorrow,
Young or old, it doesn't matter,
Let's all live together, happy ever after.

Evelyn McFadzean/Amy McFadzean

With Her

When I am with her this I know
I need to touch and hold her so
to hear her say she'll ease
this pain
I thought would never come again.

I love her face, her voice, her smile
and carry them with me all the while
and with a hope
touched by fear
dream that she might want
me near.

But once again I do but dream
and in the light of day I see
these things can never really be
and as so many times before
she's just a friend and nothing more

And so once more I turn away
towards that long awaited day
when I can find someone to see
some small thing
to love in me.

Edward B Evans

Goodnight My Someone

Someone,
Somewhere,
Sometimes,
We all feel ~ Lonely.

But just remember to say
Goodnight my someone,
Every night,
And you'll never be alone,
Again.

So goodnight my someone,
Somewhere out there,
And remember to come to me sometime
Soon!

Jonathan P Heath

The Divide

Life is a battlefield in my head
trying to fight the fear and the dread
trying to stop the falling of tears
suppressed and built up over years and years

The world can be kind ~ it can be cruel
sometimes it seems never to care at all
it seems so big ~ so impossible
for one like me to make a difference at all
But what can I do with all my thoughts and emotions
filling me up like water in the oceans
~ they bog me down
~ making me feel like I shall drown

What people do to each other
~ some of them shall never recover
In the name of love some are battered
then try and pretend it never mattered

In the name of progress lots get rich and wealthy
~ whilst others cannot even afford to stay healthy

But it doesn't matter if there is a divide
Just so long as you are on the right side

Lorna Marlow

Weightcare ~ Slimmer Of The Year

It was January 4th 2001
when Alison told me what she had done
Surprisingly entered for Slimmer Of The Year
I'll need a fat photo of you my dear

My story began on Millennium Eve
celebrating with friends Gail and Steve
Gail's dad had been filming all through the night
when I viewed the tape, 'oh what a fright!

My backside was 'wiggling' in front of Jim's face
games, fun and laughter going on in the place
In glorious colour filling the screen
I wanted to cry, I wanted to scream

The person I saw was big, fat and bloated
enough for that night Steve to be quoted
'Use the wide angle lens, Jimmy,' he said,
'That's what you'll need, it's bigger than her head.'

Embarrassed, humiliated, was I really that fat?
Surely I don't really look like that
A poem I penned to see if I could win
free classes at Weightcare to help me to slim

I received a letter to say I had won
this is where my weight loss begun
In less than 12 months I've lost 4 stone 7
I feel like I've died and gone to heaven

Friends and my family have kept me on track
each Thursday they ask me when I come back
How much have you lost, mum? Well, that's really good
you know you are eating the things that you should

I've now reached target, 10 stone was my aim
back to wearing size 12 again
My life has changed since I started slimming
this competition is not about winning

I feel I'm a winner in more ways than one
people have noticed my pert little 'bum'
If I can inspire fat people to slim
That's enough for me, I don't need to win!

But just a note in case I do
Weightcare and Alison

I'd like to thank you!

E A Barber

That Winter's Night

It came in the darkness that winter's night
Silently falling were soft flakes of white
No sound to announce the arrival of
Those flakes of snow from high above.
On hillsides steep, down valleys grand
A blanket of white covered the land
Trees stripped bare by winter winds
Now wear a coat of snowy white
That came in the darkness that winter's night.

Cold and crisp the morning air and as
Dawn began to break the golden glow
From a rising sun, reflected colours
On fields of snow gave everywhere a warming glow.
In the distance children's voices heard
Laughing, playing games and having fun
In fields of snowy white
That came in the darkness that winter's night.

E M Brooks

The Rose

Too beautiful to even write about
Too majestic to write a prose
So magnificent with all its fragrance
So exquisite is a rose
It's been with us for such a long time
And the songs of it are far and wide
It's the most popular flower to be put in rhyme
With protection growing on its side
To prune it you must wear armour
Some welders gloves should do
That scented flower, no one can harm her
As a thorn or two goes into you
For such a marvellous well-formed flower
With delightful scent and smell
Why did our creator and its maker
Give a rose such a wicked arsenal
I've been bleeding from my wrists
I've been bleeding from my fingertips
But why is it, only heaven knows
I arch my back and cry out from my lips
'I've just got to prune that blooming rose!'

Samuel Gordon Ainsley

I Sit By My Window

I sit by my window as the world goes rushing by
And no one stops to wonder at the wherefore or the why,
I sit by my window as the evening shadows fall
And cannot really understand the meaning of it all.

I sit by my window as the sun begins to wane
And in my heart I ask myself, have I lived this day in vain?
And thinking thus, I ponder, is it true for me to say
'I have helped a fellow traveller on life's tumultuous way?'

Has a kindly deed or action by now have brought relief
To someone overburdened with misery or grief?
Can someone face life's journey now, as night comes creeping on,
Because my sympathy has helped, because the fears have gone.

And when, this night, my eyelids close in search of balming sleep,
Can I rest now in tranquillity, because from out the deep,
My hand has helped another back to where that soul should be,
Diverted from the road to Hell, now to Eternity?

I sit by my window and cannot think it so,
That I have helped God's plan along, but then I do not know,
And as the twilight filters through, to do one's level best,
Must in all truth be good enough, for God will do the rest.

Maurice Bailey

Choice

Choice, just a simple word
but can mean life or death,
Freedom, the right of choice
but you took that away
when you promised me eternal life.

You promised me never-ending treasures
but you lied,
you engulfed me with those false promises,
you said you'd give me heaven
but you put me through hell.

You say you gave me the choice
well I choose damnation over following you
so from now until the day I die
you are my enemy.

Corwin V Barber

My World

Crawly caterpillars crawl all day,
have no time to stand and say,
'What has happened to the world today?'
The pollution is spreading far and wide,
nothing to eat, nowhere to hide.

People walking, sadly sighing,
all around animals are dying,
on the ground seagulls are lying.
All over the beaches spread so far,
seals are captured in the tar.

Human beings should be ashamed
of this life that I've explained,
of all the lives that have been drained.
Stop now before it's too late
and please start cleaning up this state.

Ryan Smith (8)

The Wasp

It hovers round the apples,
And dances round the pears,
Gracefully flying round the orchard,
Searching for some food.

It finds a fallen pear,
And gently goes in to land,
Slowly it moves from side to side,
And takes back off again.

It looks like a tiny tiger,
And hums like a busy bee,
Flying like a frantic bird,
Its colours warning me.

Soon it gets into trouble
Being attacked by a giant
With a rolled up newspaper
Being hit and beaten.

It panics and turns around,
Madly dodging the shots,
It does the only thing it can,
And stings the attacker.

The attacker stops still,
And then screams aloud,
'Ouch, ouch, oww, oww.'
Then he runs away crying!

For our little wasp,
It's time for him to go,
He settles down in the grass,
To die in peace.

Scott Smith (12)

Painting A Picture Of October

Painting a picture of October
Is not difficult to do,
All those burning colours
To capture are for you.

The fiery leaves on treetops
Like maiden's auburn hair,
All the animals of winter
Are already there.

The warm bright sun bewitches you
To think it's summer time,
But the seasons are laughing at you
For thinking 'Why oh why?'

Painting October makes you happy
It does the same to me,
You'll find yourself clapping and singing
Just wait and see!

Get out your paints and easel
Shade in the darkening sky,
Acorns and pine cones hanging on the boughs
All will be waiting tomorrow right where they were today.
But now you must say farewell my friend
For it is autumn time.

Janet Marie James (10)

In This Life

In this life of chosen mind
lie embers of our past
those silhouettes that gently bind
with memories that last

Of whispered sounds in hallowed halls
bright coloured beams in waterfalls
and dragonflies, that hang in space
as frail as mist, or paper lace

Cross tranquil meadow, weaving green
by babbling brook or languid stream
where torpid willow quietly sigh
and herringbone, criss-cross the sky

That wispy cloud, like cotton frond
span endless sky, the great beyond
a life of wonders there to find
in this life, of chosen mind.

Paul Esser

The Horrid Potion

This is a potion for the sad
and also the bad
Splishing, splashing,
boiling and dashing
A chicken's bone,
and a roadwork cone,
a branch of a tree,
and a church key,
A person's sock
with a tail of a peacock,
and a shell of a snail,
with a tiger's tail,
A person's nose,
mixed in with human toes
The head of a cat
and the eye of a rat
a lot of cold rain
and a spider's brain
Splishing, splashing
boiling and dashing
A shark's tooth,
and don't forget the house roof
Splishing and splashing
boiling and dashing.

Owen Fleming (10)

Love

Brave skeletons, kerb crawling
On the frosted voyage
Of capricious dreams
On which we necessitate
Fibrous castles

Cinderella's shoeless complex
A black crow on Van Gogh canvas
An epitaphic blunder of
A Shakespearean fantasy
No one questions you
Only the vacant chambers
In the heartless wishbones

This pain
That graveyard
An abused honour
It's a circumcised ray
Trapped in shadows
A fire caught on smokes
A purple taste on Flamingo craving
The lust driven on
The chariots of tantric doldrums
A devil in white quartz disguise

O love you're an angel
Placed in the wings of
A blinded Unicorn

Seema Gill

Mother

It's no wonder
They call this planet
Old Mother Earth
Because you've been my world
From the day of my birth
You love and protect me
And show that you care
If things go wrong
I know that you're there
To help me and guide me
To show me the way
How to put things right
At the end of the day
We all make mistakes
People point and they sneer
But when we turn round
We know you'll be there
To pick up the pieces
Be strong, never sway
This is a debt
We can never repay
All the perfume
The flowers, chocolates too
Can never quite say
What we think of you
We all love you dearly
And thank you each day
For making life's path
An easier way

John Flanagan

My Old Town

There used to be a Paper mill out where a Hotel stands.
And what became an Office block used to be the Theatre Grand.
I used to think that Hospitals were built on sacred ground.
Until the so-called hand of progress brought them tumbling down.

Tumbling down.

Now thinking about the house of prayer and the School that I'd
attend.
How they made way for a car park to meet some fresh demand.
And I'm thinking about my children and the things we're handing
down
Nothing more than memories and dreams of my old Town.

Now the old Black Bear's a cycle track, and the Brewery's long gone
And they've built another retail park, like we need another one.
We've fun pubs that ain't funny, but I guess that's nothing new.
While traffic lights and ring roads try to keep us on the move.

On the move.

Oh I'm thinking about the fun we had in the days when children
could.
Hitching rides on the swinging bridges, camping out in dingle woods.
And I'm thinking about my own kids and the things we're handing
down
Nothing more than photographs and tears for my old town.
Nothing more than memories and dreams of my old town.

My old town.

John Birch

The Tree Of Life

Trees, are truly wondrous things
A refuge there, for birds on wings
Where they can just perch and rest
Or, maybe there, they'll build their nest
Berries on them provide food
So that they can feed their brood
Their cycle, really helps us see
How new life, can come to be
Their leaves, wither, die, and fall
But, the wonder of it all
Is there, to be seen by all
Just a few months, after 'fall'
New buds, and foliage, in the spring
Hope of new life, to all, will bring
A truly wonderful thing to see
And only God, can make a tree

Joyce Metcalfe

Contentment

The list of things she didn't possess,
The skills which weren't within her range,
Her friends all thought her powerless,
Acquaintances thought her quite strange.

'No car?' they asked, 'no microwave,
Washing machine, nor answerphone?
Computerless? No means to save
Yourself from hours at home alone?'

'Why no,' she said, 'I need them not,
I'm rich and do without them all.
I miss them not one tiny jot,
And don't forget, my bills are small!'

'I have the things which matter most ~
My home, my health, my friends who care.
And more than all, I have my God
Who day by day is always there.'

Eleanor M Parker

Black Mountain And Its Valleys

A mountain that changes its distance view,
Mist slowly rising up to the sun,
Snow-capped ridges in winter months,
Streams trickling down in summer days,
A sheep softly grazing as you walk by,
Blue skies and the heather on the mountain top,
To Hereford Ross many counties you see,
It's a view, if clear, is never forgot.

Trees all around not changed for many a day,
A moorhen, a fish or birds flying high,
Brooks softly running down valleys nearby
Covered in scented white blossom, the hawthorn in May,
All through the valleys its beauty unfold,
And its red berries feed the birds in the winter cold,
Around every corner a different view,
Winding lanes, adventure for you,
Peace and a welcome to stop and stare,
Beauty untold for us all to share.

Sylvia Farr

Greed

The darkest cloud that destroys the day,
Is when greed and power dictate the way
Darkness surrounds a troubled soul,
When material things we make the goal
Why! Because, you see my friend,
We just can't take it in the end
One can't accumulate and save,
It doesn't fit within the grave.

Rich man has never seen God's light,
As he's grappled for money from morning till night
Never had time to take in God's power,
Of reasons and wonder supplied every hour
Never had true friends to help him to live,
Or the joy in the heart of learning to give
He sees no bright sky at the end of hard day,
Contentment and peace just don't come his way.

Ignorance and poverty stem from greed,
They shouldn't, God created, to supply every creed
Sustenances and trust and love,
In such great measure come from above
He hoped that we would do the same,
As homeward bound we walk life's lane
As you go through life don't hide your light
Always strive to do what's right.

The love and knowledge passed on from you,
Comes back in abundance from our God so true
By radiant smile and contented look,
We follow the wisdom of His holy book
For as you give, so you shall receive,
When our earthly life we have to leave
The examples you have set below,
Are known by God as to Him you go.

Edna Bainbridge

The Apple Tree

We grow old together, the tree and I
Bark peels from a trunk holed by generations of woodworm
The lichened branches grey like the colour of my hair.
It stands, bare branches a tracery against the wintry sky.
A silent sentinel on watch.

It has been there a hundred years or more
Was there when we moved into the cottage many years ago
What tales it could tell of days gone by.

Each spring blossoms cascade down in breathtaking beauty
On branches that sweep down to the ground.
The tits, wagtails, robins, blackbirds use the branches
As springboards for the bird table close by.

I look back across the years to the pram beneath its branches
See the waving hands, kicking feet and hear chortles of mirth
As the baby tries to catch the fluttering leaves.

I feel again the warmth of the dappled sun as I lay on the grass
Beneath its green canopy and
Hear again the laughter of friends as we dine Victorian style
Beneath the boughs.

I see again the abundance of apples in the Autumn and
Hear their plop, plop as the wind blows them to the ground and
Hear the rustle of the autumn leaves as they skip and dance
In the gentle breeze.

Oh lovely tree, stay there forever watching over me
When I am gone stay on and watch over all who come after.
Oh lovely tree, stay forever.

Mary D Woodman

A Husband's Lament

My wife knows what's best for me
She often tells me so
If I mention going for a drink
She quickly says 'Oh no' not whilst there's dishes in the sink

Then there's the weekly shopping trip
As I push the trolley round
I see the items mounting up
Watch my money go
Who eats it all I'll never know

Evening comes and we settle down
Upon the old settee
I put my arm about her waist or maybe touch her knee
She sits quite still for just a minute
Then decides we want some tea

Sadly as I watch her go
And think of what might be
I know deep down within my heart
My wife does *not* know what's best for me

R M Dodds

Devon Sunset

Streaks of orange and crimson
Behind a smudge of grey
An unearthly whiteness between them
Heralding the close of day.
The sheep are blobs like shadows
Beneath the ominous trees
Gaunt, black and foreboding
On their carpet, now olive green.
A grey-black Gothic spire
Pierces the blood-streaked sky
And the stream meanders in silence
Mourning the death of day.

Iris Reeves Williams

Heroes

We all have heroes, Dads; Stars; Friends,
We want to grow up to be like them,
But what if we can't for as we learn to worship,
They're stolen from us ~ Plucked in their prime,
Taken from this place, from this world,
To live their lives anew, afresh,
Eternity in a gem,
Leaving us to get on with our lives,
In pain, in danger, in sorrow,
In tears, the pain goes after an eternity,
And then you find yourself thinking,
'What would he do if they were here now?'
And as you live your life through them,
Doing as they would and did,
The memory lives on forever, and the guilt,
Why couldn't you have gone too?

James Kinsey (15)

Winter

The winter blues are on us
The summer's gone away
We sit in our chairs and wonder
What we can do today
The wind is blowing, the rain is falling
So what are we going to do
Just wrap up warm with hats and coats
And hope we don't catch the flu

Val Nichols

Sorrow

The church is full of people weeping,
People crying for the dying,
Mothers, fathers, children too,
They all know someone who,
Has perished in the big earthquake,
Why them they say,
What have they done?
No one can understand,
They all pray for a miracle,
In this ill-fated land.

Rosalie McDuffus

Time To Stop

I see the beauty all around,
in the trees, the sky ~ even in the ground.
But why do we do our best to destroy,
the things put on earth for us to enjoy?
We pollute the sky with toxic waste,
cut down the trees to make more space.
Build roads of tarmac for miles and miles
taking away the fields I played on, as a child.
It's time to stop this slaughter of our home,
give back the fields and the woods where we roamed,
with life abundant and flowers to see,
this could once be again a place of beauty.
Give our children a chance of a life we once had,
free from the smoke and smut that comes for a cab.
Slow down the progress, let the earth take a rest,
let the air be clean as we take our next breath.
So no more destruction of the earth's natural things,
let Mother Nature start her healings.
If we do this now before it's too late,
this world that we know will be a far better place.

Victor James Gunstone

Idyll

The skein and tangle of the autumn leaves
Rich, crisp and yellow with a russet tint;
Two swallows nesting on the rooftop eaves,
The scented flavours of the garden's mint
The shrill-pitched music of the skylark's song,
Clear rushing water as it flows along,
Between the banks of thyme and willow tree;
The curved down softness of the royal swans
Sailing majestic on a placid mirror
Untroubled by the murmuring of human tongues
Or the rocking ripples of a passing steamer
Green grass caressed by gentle winds
And moist with touches of a scented dew
Near where the spider weaves and spins
His threaded muslin on the churchyard yew.

Dennis A Brunning

Holiday In Pembrokeshire

This land's alive! In vale and hill
the quickening spirit lingers still
of saints, whose holy feet have trod
a landscape to th' incarnate God;

their tracks and paths, linked vertebrae,
each sun-bleached bone a pilgrim's way,
whose broken signposts seek to guide
our steps to places sanctified.

This land's alive! breathes everywhere
the perfume of life-giving prayer,
while every sainted cwm and bay
invites us to make holy day.

Denis Parry

Dragon's Breath

A dragon's breath is hot and red
If it breathes on you you're dead
So when you see one flying by
On the ground you must lie
You must lie very still
Don't move or see you he will
If he sees you, down he'll come
Then you must run run run
Head for somewhere you can hide
Somewhere narrow not wide
So he can't get in not even his head
'Cos if he breathes on you you're dead

J Annetts

Moon Thoughts

The moonlight on the garden shines
Covering plants and garden gnomes alike
With a gentle soft silvery light
That dreams are made of.

I lie in bed amid the dark
There's creaks and groans, sometimes dogs bark,
Imagination starts to work
And nervousness begins to come, creeping in.

Then peeping through my curtains clear
Bright moonlight chases all my fear,
And calm I lie and dream of things
Like holidays, love and golden rings.

J Robertson

My Wandering Spirit

Before I go to sleep at night
I close my eyes and pray
And as I'm drifting into sleep
My Spirit slips away

Off into the Spirit World
To meet old friends and new
Wandering off to see the sights
As it's such a wonderful view

The sky is clear blue overhead
With continuous sunshine
And the flowers in the gardens here
Are enough to blow your mind

I see mountains in the background
And a sparkling waterfall
I swear I came here with problems
But it appears I've forgotten them all

For this is a beautiful place to be
With a friendly atmosphere
Such beauty is often hard to find
Such friendliness so rare

It seems a shame to have to leave
But I know I must go back
To where my body lies asleep
Where everything seems black

And when I wake in the morning
I know I'll feel at peace
Knowing that is where I'll live
When my life here has to cease

Rosemarie Bruce

A Gosling's Breast

A red egg in a gosling's breast,
A ball of mountain fire,
Low beyond the peach pink dawn,
A gosling etched in black desire.

A calm blue wave crests her black outline,
A dried leaf holds her black bubble,
The castle's flag flaps a pennant of love,
And keeps a bird in flight from trouble.

The dried leaf, a brown crisp etch,
It holds a ruby tear,
Where a star and sun float beneath its vein,
Outlines a tale I cannot hear.

A smaller leaf covers a purple hue,
Coloured by pencil and hand,
But the brown small arc I cannot tell,
But a whiter lie, and a faint tinged hand.

The eye doesn't leap with the soul,
To see beyond the pencilled hand,
But feels its path so rough, on smooth
Until one's guess does turn to sand.

C A Brown

Autumn

Crunchy ruby leaves
falling to the ground
branches creak
birds migrate
ochre leaves
dance around
but the trees
are all lonely
very sad
with no
friends around
wind is weeping
as golden leaves
float around
saffron veils
riding through
a beautiful
forest with
wishing grass.

Jade Murphy Symonds (7)

Angels

Angel of the morning
sing your song for me
bring sunshine back into my life
the way it used to be.

Angel of the noontime
ease my aching heart
yearning for the one I love
for we now live apart.

Angel of the evening
weave your magic charms
and bring my lover back to me
to my ever waiting arms.

Angel of the night time
do not cry for me
for I have grown old waiting
and now face eternity.

I must make my mind up
do I live or die
angel of tomorrow
perhaps you'll tell me *why*

Patricia Brett

No News
(May 19th 1989)

I don't want to hear the news today
Won't listen to others views
'bout the spread of Aids, or current shades of World War Three
For today is mine

As a gentle breeze soothes
this hot-tempered world
And the seeds are all stretching new leaves which uncurl
From the womb of the rich dark earth

In the still of last night came gentle moans
from the meadow outside my room
In the dawn lay a newly born calf, bathed in his mother's pride
(He took his first steps in the world today . . .)

Some fledglings are making first flights overhead
and I've called my dog back ~ just in time
For a sleepy small rabbit to disappear . . .
Out of harm's way . . . So no news today

Carole E Drew

Aurora

The sun will rise as never before,
Its radiant brilliance promising more.
Purpose flows into those below.
Lighting up their lives.
Rejuvenated, they will rise in glory,
For this is the new world,
Where anything is possible.
And everything is probable.

Or so they are told.

They can be happy, they can feel,
Their lives can be joyful,
They can be real.
Hopes and dreams will be realised,
Fears and doubts will be banished,
The truth in life will be seized.

But then they increase the heat.

The searing sun will sting their eyes,
The painful shine signals demise;
As nature decrees the end of all.
Bodies slowly corrupt and decay,
The scorched remnants simmer away.
Mindless slaughtering destroys all hope,

As the world goes by in a flash of tears.

Twisted scenes of stillborn dreams,
The corpses left to haunt the rest.
Shrilling cries, persistent lies,
They mutilate each other.
They'll continue to discriminate,
To fill this bloody world with hate;
To rape all trust (they will, they must).
It's natural.

We're human.

Martin J MacInnes

Helping Hand

When you wake up in the morning
Make the most of each new day
Tell yourself you will do your utmost
To help someone on the way
Someone who needs a helping hand
Who needs a word of cheer
Perhaps it will help someone
Whose life is very drear.
Show the world you are ready
Put a smile upon your face
Hold your heart and hand steady
In this rushing, pushing human rat race.

Mary Whittaker

Anglesey

When I was a pagan island
formed of mists,
Priests trod my hills and glades.
Cloud fields covered me with dark drapes,
my straits were proud and thundered hard.
Bards sang of my freedom everywhere.
Druids wrote it on mossy urns,
upon tapestries on rare manuscripts
a thousand ways.

To the stilled stone tumult
of my brooding land the Romans came ashore.
They trampled underfoot my sacred groves.
Stripped to the bone my pagan joys.
Yet, there must be another spring
for new blades green, new hopes.
When earth's dark furrowed brow relaxes and gives
back my ancient
Holly, that blossoms out of death.

Alan Hougardy

Dreams

Dreams, we know not what they are,
They can be liken to a star
That shines in the sky so bright.
They glisten then only at night.
Dreams appear only during sleep
When the sky is in darkness deep,
Awaken then in the morning
Wondering about those images dawning.
When awake they seem faded
Just sleepy memories jaded,
With day again ready to start
Think of that with all your heart.

Iris E Weller

A Blanket Of Darkness

Rain spilled thunder roared
Clouds huddled together for comfort
Fear and pain turned to torment
Cries to anguished screams
Cloaked in a blanket of darkness
When blackness engulfed the skies
Emptiness replacing life

Maura Rea

Beyond Love

Outward through space
Between
A difference this space

Explanation

Search between objects
Moving and still

Between walls

Space enclosed within walls
Within space that surrounds
Between moving still surrounds

Temporary time spent
Having resonance
Unoccupied by others so filled

Travelling movement
Leaving order
Delightful disorder
Dreaming through mountains seen
Sat upon that edged lake washed
Uneven shore

Only home so loved
Without walls to confine
Surrounded embrace
Felt of space

Outward

The time remembered
From that first place of exit
Synapse rebound
And a glow in your unpresence

Taken flight
Words of distance
Held then and there
Upon the outline of nothingness
A reminder of the unremembered

M Belton

The Rose

All alone. Alone in the room.
My eyes fixed firmly on the rose bud beginning to bloom.
I see the dainty red petals curved with grace,
And glance in the mirror by my side,
At the face full of hurt, that I tried to hide.
Turning sadly at the rose for a second glance,
I stared at its features in a peculiar trance.
It shone with such beauty before my helpless sight,
That I hadn't even encountered in any dreams at night.
It confused me, that I hadn't realised,
The extravagant species before my eyes.

The red rose is a symbol of devoted love,
Gleaming with joy like an angel from the heavens above.
I dream and sometimes pray that everyone knows,
That true love only lies deep inside the heart of a,
Red, red rose.

Jennifer Ferguson (17)

Untitled

So much He has to give
in this life where we now live
He is the one who is, who was, and is to come.
The way, the truth, the life,
His redeeming blood paid the price
for a richer, fuller way of life.
Life to the full, no holds barred
is why my Jesus He was marred.
Despite the pain and the shame,
He gave His life that we may gain
life complete, riches untold
victory over sin and death
to loosen us from Satan's hold.

Lyn Spencer

The Mighty Power

Miniature threads of gleaming azure
Pittering and pattering.

Long and winding
Snaking through the countryside,
Rippling, splashing
Pittering and pattering.

Like a serpent approaching its prey
Moving faster, gathering speed,
Travelling, rushing
Rippling, splashing
Pittering and pattering.

Always pursuing its final goal,
Covering distances
Chapters of life.
Speeding, dashing,
Travelling, rushing
Rippling, splashing
Pittering and pattering.

Finally reaching its destination
Cold and dark,
Open and free
Joining the brilliance of the blueness,
Intensity growing, pressure building
Searching, roaming,
Speeding, dashing,
Travelling, rushing
Rippling, splashing
Pittering and pattering.

The mighty power of the *river*.

Kerry Byng

Have You Ever?

Have you ever heard anything,
 Anything at all,
That sounds as calm and soft,
 As a summer night's breeze?

Have you ever seen anything,
 Anything at all,
That looks as elegant and graceful,
 As a dove, white swan?

Have you ever smelt anything,
 Anything at all,
That smells as sweet and beautiful,
 As the dew on the early morning flowers?

 I have!

 Michelle Gray (12)

Memories

My age brings happy memories
Of years so long ago;
Of rows of little houses,
All standing in a row.
Of mother, father, brother
And friends at school, at play;
With such happy memories,
They come to me each day.

A back to back we lived in,
No garden or a yard.
We never felt, as children,
Or knew, that times were hard.
We'd play whip-top and marbles,
Or round the streets we'd run,
With skipping rope or 'go cart';
So simple, but such fun.

No bathroom in the old days,
But a tin bath on the rug;
The lovely coal fire burning,
The room so warm and snug;
A fireguard always in its place,
The fender shining bright;
A dry, a hug, from Mum and Dad
And a kiss to say, 'goodnight.'

And what about our music?
A wind-up gramophone;
'Til they invented wireless;
'Be quiet,' Dad would moan.
He'd let us put the earphones on,
We'd join, 'twas only fair.
That orchestra was magic,
How did they get in there?!

No other generation
Has seen such changes made:
Such wonderful inventions;
But memories never fade.
I may be in a cosy flat
My parents would adore,
But I shan't forget their love for us;
And bless them evermore.

Mary Singleton McLelland

Nature

Nature restores me to myself
Dries the tears from my eyes,
She soothes my mind in times of grief
And turns my troubles and my sighs
    To sweet relief
    Everlasting.
From turmoiled towns
    Insanity and restlessness
To flowering dreams in wilderness
And memories of delightful youth,
When time meant nought,
And money could not buy that peace
We search vainly for today
    And find it not.
And innocence of love we knew
    Exists no more.

Jamie Lawrence Curtis

Sun

Oh, how we regard you, celestial light
We worship your heat, you reward us with sight
Ninety-three million miles distant, yet our nearest star
Your heavenly rays, we collect from afar

The life on this planet, and the elements, of course
Are put down to you, our one creative source
We're always conscious of subtle shade and hue
Which are wrapped up in colour, a spectrum of you

Expression is hard of the thoughts that I feel
You hold us together, our very life's seal
We love all thy energy, dispersed every day
You know what you're doing in your own precise way

Great golden globe, you fill the Earth with power
Pertaining to strength, then, you are our tower
You are the centre of our collective whole
Long life for the Earth is our central goal

Such are your movements from East through to West
We watch you with pleasure your host to our guest
Sunrise is beauty, a new day appears
With sunset we part, tomorrow, no fears.

Thomas William Cameron

Nobody In Particular

If I close my eyes and count to ten
   Would you still be there when I look again
If we parted ways, would you be sad
   Or would you walk way, and not look back
If I left tonight would you still be fine
   Would you write to me, if you had the time
If we never spoke, would you forget my name
   And if I returned, would things be the same
If I asked for help, would you be by my side
   And if I needed you, would you be hard to find
If I walked in pain, could I count on you
   And if I had a burden, would you share it too
If I count to ten and close my eyes
   When I give you this, will you read it twice?

Lauri Love

New Year's Eve 2000

Around the world
a new year revolves
second by second
bit by bit
sweeping dimly.
The new dawning of an ordinary day
an aurora of hope and forgetfulness.
And yet
I still hope all
and forget nothing.
I hope for a new future . . .
a beginning again . . .
a revolution that this time
will resolve positively,
will evolve your love,
will solve our problem,
will involve us,
together.

Kate Woodruff

Prancer

She came to us one Autumn time, this bundle full of fun,
With such a personality, she was second to none.

So pleased at last to have a home, she gave us so much love,
An extrovert in every way, yet gentle as a dove.

The presents on our doorstep came, a frankfurter, no less,
A lamb's heart, then an eyeless fish, from where we could not guess.

We weren't so sure about the rat that stayed out on the drive,
She couldn't get it through the gate ~ at least it wasn't live!

She didn't have the best of health throughout the years to come,
But always warmly welcomed us whenever we came home.

She had her favourite places to watch the world go by,
A trug when in the garden, a window sill up high.

She loved to play with leaves and she would prance across the lawn
The catnip plants could not survive her nibbles ~ they got torn!

Indoors she had a tennis ball, this feline roly-poly,
She'd beat it up, and chase it, but she'd never make a goalie.

She had her special sleeping spots, a cat's bed wouldn't do,
She liked Mum's lap, and her armchair ~ conservatory too.

For on a sunny day she'd stretch right out, and there she'd stay,
And, in the winter, by the fire was where she'd like to lay.

We miss her now her time's run out ~ no tap upon the door
To let us know she's had her walk and she is home once more.

We miss her at the start of day, the 'Brr' that said 'Hello',
The way she loved her brush and comb ~ she revelled in it so.

But we are grateful for her life and all the joy we shared,
We miss you so, our Prancer, but know you knew we cared.

Jose Evelyn

A Dignified Silence

A dignified silence, is that all that's left
When all confessions have dried up
What's to do but say less
Is a dignified silence the most civilised mode
When six years of unity hits a fork in the road

Best you stare at your wall
I'll stare at mine
See a collage of good times
No water, all wine.

A dignified silence, is this sensible, most wise,
To leave the sadness and anger
In our hearts and our eyes
A dignified silence is no adolescent state
We're rational adults, handling ill-fated fate.

Best you stare at your wall
I'll stare at mine
See a collage of good times
No hatred, no crimes.

A dignified silence can mask the bitterness and pain,
From harsh words and fighting no solace we gain.

Best you stare at your wall,
I'll stare at mine
See a collage of good times
No Shakespearean tragedy, just pure pantomime.

A dignified silence, that's all we possess,
After running the whole gamut
From delight to this sorry mess.

Best you stare at your wall
I'll stare at mine
Embrace our good times
As we hit this divide.

Phil Jones

The Friesan

She lifts her head to sniff the air
A momentary pause from grass
(Who is sat on *her* wall?)
She is strong.

Her mouth descends to grass again
And rips it, tears it, munches it
She moves;
One foot forward, another slowly following.

Full, pink udders swaying
Tail flicking at unseen flies
She is graceful
With her powerful muddy haunches.

Moving slowly, now stopped
Now standing still, ears pricked up
She is listening;
Her black and white hide stark against the grass.

A bass guttural sound
A primitive call, a solid sound
She is talking;
The sound too base for such a graceful creature.

She turns and plods away
Slowly following her plodding sisters
Slowly, so slowly she leaves me behind
Her warm breath rising in the evening air.

Jill Wilmore

War Of Freedom

When war is coming
There'll be no running
There's only fighting to satisfy man.
Think of the future.
What can it bring you?
Only the heartache of losing your man.

It happens all the world over.
For every colour and creed.
If you wipe out a race
It will be a disgrace.
So let all men be freed.

Woman praying there'll be no killing.
Their men sleeping out in the cold.
Hoping that one day,
One day soon
They'll be home before they are old.

It's all the same the world over.
So join our Company.
We work all day,
We pray all night,
That our men will soon be free.

Women crying, their men dying.
Baby is sleeping there in his bed.
Men are slaying for their freedom.
For their freedom?
But now they are dead.

Linda Wright

Church

A strong face of wood and stone
Upon the hill standing alone
An earthen path runs to the door
Braced with iron and standing sure
Through an arch into the nave
Shaded pews sombre and grave
Along the aisle to take a seat
Dressed smart and trim and calm and neat
Sometimes the church attracts an age
Of social form to the proper stage

A smile a laugh a twinkling eye
An open hall to reach the sky
Chair and table spread about
Free to the air for inside is out
Soft skeins and fills to deck the cloth
Colours bright delicate and soft
Flowers and petals ribbons and bows
Exhibiting freedom each child here knows
Sometimes the church is of an age
Where freedom and light is all the rage

Whether 'proper' or 'free' the church has its role
Keeping the children it cares for quite whole
Either formal or fresh the church has its place
To welcome all those who seek out its grace
To help us poor sinners to find our way
And turn sorrow to smiles at the end of the day
The church is for people to worship and prayer
Our Lord God in heaven will rejoice with us there
So let us feel lightness either proper or free
And Jesus' love flow unto you and to me.

NJM

The Game

It's a game
It's all the same
day after day
A life, death, and rain
blame it on the rain

Same old same old same
win or lose
join, cheat or play
Delete, retreat
And blame it on the game.

Play,
draw, shoot and regain
your stance
play your chance
enhance your brain
And blame it on the game.

Roll your dice
your choice, your vice
your life
remain the same
and blame it on
The game.

Rob Mears

Never-Ending Love

I would blaze a trail across the cosmos
Just to hold you in my arms, as you're my
Crimson rose in a field of yellow orchids.
And when my heart is in despair I close
My eyes and dream of you, as the feelings
I have for you I can no longer hide.
Your love ignites my heart, your smile glows
Inside me like a firefly at night. We would stand together
Under a moonlit sky as I taste your sweet lips on mine
The stars would sparkle through your eyes
As my heart beats faster for a passion for which I thirst for
And when you're sad and lonely I would let my tears fall
Like drops upon your body to cool your flames of sadness.
My only wish is for you and a love that never ends.

Charles Hepburn

Skywalking

It's a dangerous thing to sit and dream on Morvern
Beneath the flimsy clouds and speeding sky
For dreams are like the stuff the clouds are made of
They change their shape and spread their wings and fly

Beware of lying down on Ardnamurchan
And listening to the curlew's plaintive sound
The sky will steal your soul and make a run for it
And leave your body empty on the ground

I sat and mused for hours on Ardgour pasture
And vaguely heard the cuckoo's distant song
I wandered in my mind along the mountains
And came back down and found that I had gone

Wendy Grant

The Man

I, will never be like you.
I, as open, forthright, true.
As you, are covered in,
a second skin.
The real essence,
hidden far below,
rarely,
if ever allowed to show.
Fearing your serpent's tongue,
(lisping, scenting)
should repulse,
those,
you hope to attract,
then destroy
firstly having used.
enjoyed.

Stevie

Touch Not My Soul

Touch not my soul but with a gentle hand
Like the fragile wings of butterfly or moth
Singed by life's harsh candle flame, storm-tossed
It cannot now those cruel winds withstand

But should the storms cease and the winds abate
And life's bruising cacophony recede
And sun turn spider webs to filaments of gold
Then my soul will heal before it is too late

Valerie Atkins

A Complex Woman

Some say she is gregarious
To others she's a bore
With some she is quite serious
For many she's a chore

Some say that she's voluptuous
While others find her fat
Some say her clothes are sumptuous
For many they are tat

Some say that she is upper class
To others she's a slag
With many she's a gentle lass
To some she is a hag

Some say that she lights up a room
And sparkles with great wit
With some she sprinkles doom and gloom
And does not seem to fit

Trying to define her is very hard to do
Lots of different people there
Unique as morning dew

Heather M Marsland

Dreams

'O I love cats,' the little boy said,
As he stroked every cat he could find,
'When I grow up I'll have one.'
But he didn't know
The fact that he'd grow
Would probably change his mind

I could see he was serious
From the things that he said,
But when all's said and done
And he wants to have fun
He'll grow up and do things instead

He'll find football and pubs,
Girls, cars and clubs,
Much more attractive than now
He'll go out for smokes
With the other blokes,
The cat long forgotten somehow

Skateboarding and cycling,
Kissing or fighting,
He'll all too soon be a man
And I wonder if then
He'll remember his dream
I wonder if anyone can

Diana Price

In Memory

Slowly gazing around the room,
She tries to see through the twilight gloom.
Her mind travels back through the mists of time,
Sweet memories of her past to find.

Of days spent in the summer sun,
Days full of friends all having fun.
A little girl in her Sunday best,
Eager to be seen, eager to impress.

Mother and daughter strolling down the street,
Smiling, greeting everyone they meet.
Then it's off back home to the Sunday roast,
Where father makes a solemn toast.

'We think of those who have gone before,
Those who have passed through Heaven's door.
We think of those who have yet to go,
May the Angels guide them, show them where to go.'

Many glorious years have passed by,
It's always surprising how fast time does fly.
It's sad to see that all has changed,
To her the world at large seems strange.

Slowly she raises her weary head,
To see who stands beside her bed.
Her heart is full, a warm golden glow,
It seems that now it's her time to go.

Gracefully she rises highly
Higher and higher into the sky.
Closely following that leading light,
All that was, now, out of sight.

Today she'll follow that path well used before,
Today she'll pass through Heaven's door.
Again there'll be days of happiness in the sun,
Friends together all having fun.

E M Evans

In The Millennium

In the millennium I . . .
Like to Dance
I like to Prance
I like to make Mince Pies

I like to Burp
I like to Slurp
I like to do Gym

I like to Look
I like a Book
I like to bake a Chocolate Cake.

I like . . . I like . . . I like . . . I like . . . I like the *millennium*

Sammi Walsh (9)

Mother

She sits alone, beneath the giant canopy of trees,
Shaded from a sun more intense than she's known for a while.
Shedding tears, once pure, now tainted with the dirt of an age.
Where did I go wrong, asks Mother, like mothers before and since.
I gave them love and warmth and food ~ not enough,
Never enough.
They always wanted more.
And the fights, the arguments ~
Why can't they just be, and be happy with what they have.
Where did their contentment go?
Were they ever really content, or did I just wish that for them?
Oh my children, you never visit me anymore,
Never think of me or the harm you do.
You've forgotten your way to me over the mists of time ~
Got too clever,
Too sophisticated.
The old ways forgotten, buried in shrouds of ignorance . . .
A movement catches her gaze.
And then another,
Far away.
Well, well, after all this time?
A visitor, and more than one ~
They struggle to break through, the journey long and hard,
For some more than others.
But they'll get there.
We'll get there . . .
But will it be too late?
Regrets.
Opportunities lost.

Helen McGregor

To My Valentine

When you found me
I was an island
Surrounded by a sea of despair
A ship in a storm
Tossed by turbulent waves
Of grief, betrayal and loss.

I was running scared
Crying out for help
Without knowing where to turn
And then I found you ~ my calm in the storm.

Our first meeting ~ tentative, shy
Wanting to trust, but with hearts
Still bleeding from recent wounds.
Yearning to be close, yet holding back
In case the hopes each held
Proved false, as so many times before.

Two lonely souls, coming to terms
With the pain inflicted by past shadows
Wanting to move on, yet holding back.
Fearful of making the first step
~ what if, once more, the dagger was poised
To draw more blood from an ever-deepening wound?

But as time has moved on
We are learning to trust once more
To believe the love we have discovered
Can calm the stormy waters of the past.
The dark nights are fading now ~
And our love will be like a candle
Guiding us toward the light.

Together we are moving away from the hurt
Which has shadowed us for so long.
And we will go forward to discover a
World full of light and hopes and dreams ~
Our world of everlasting love.

Sue Southgate

Washing Day

I opened my washing machine
And saw to my great surprise
The handkerchiefs, shirts and skirts,
Whatever the shape or size
Of the garments,
Had all turned blue!
White-blue and blue-white,
Blue-grey and grey-blue,
What to do?
The wrong colours all gave a disguise
To the contents and use
Of the objects.
My husband's white undies
And various sundries
Were tinted and flecked in new hue.
My negligee may be faded and frayed
But is now a tired white, edged in blue:
The poses of roses look wilted and jilted,
And I fear that's the way they will stay.

I reached for the bleach and cold water,
And stuck all the clothes in to soak,
I poked and I stroked, I rinsed and I winced,
As my hands became rougher ~ skin broke!
By lunchtime the clothing hung high,
On the horse, in the kitchen to dry:
There's fantastic elastic,
Bright blue on the white,
And blue lace on the base of my slip.
My bra is a sight
Half sky-blue, half white,
But nothing's quite spoilt by its dip!

Shirley Boyce

Youth

If only I were young again
Young and fancy free
Having not a care in the world
And no responsibility

But youth is wasted on the young
For that is the belief
When we are young, we have no concept
Of what life can really be

Wisdom is something that is acquired
As we grow old graciously
If I knew then, what I know now
Is spoken repeatedly

So I'll be content that I am older
And wiser with a wealth of experience
For life is but a learning path
All the way out of existence

Phyllis Stark

Just Twenty-Four Hours

The rising sun turns red, the dawn's pale glow.
A church clock chimes, the farmyard cockerels crow.
Now stirs the village, the hour of daylight breaks.
A barking dog, the cottage light, the countryside awakes.
Workers, housewives, farmers, early starts the day.
Children safely now at school, the toddlers home at play.
Busy pass the working hours. 'Off to the village hall'
A most important visit! ~ The WI's market stall.
Impetuous winds, now clouds go scudding by.
Honking skeins of flying geese noisily fills the sky.
The long day closes, the people homeward bound.
Again the church clock chimes the hour, a peaceful village sound.

M Cadman

An Invitation

Come down in the deep,
Watch crabs crawl and creep,
Octopus asleep
Legs wave with the tide.

Come down in the deep,
And now with me keep
Watching fish leap
And twirl with the tide.

Cath Little

Grandad

One cold wet dark November day,
God came and took a loved one away,
To sit beside him in the sky.
So he can watch over us from on high.
To guide us with a helping hand.
A man who never did do any wrong.
Peacefully he lies remembered by everyone.
For all the things he's done, a man to be respected,
Someone who'll be missed, a man who gave so very much.
Strong in his beliefs, gentle with his words,
A faith, which will lead him to the light.
Into the arms of those who went before,
United, resting at the right hand of the Lord.

John Leslie Pearson

Sunshine

Sunshine in the garden,
Sunshine in the street.
Sunshine all this morning,
Sunshine all this week.

Sun, sun is lots of fun,
I play in it all the time.
I wish that it was always there
And I wish that it was mine.

Kirsten Somerville (9)

Tell Me

Tell me,
What would it mean
If words
Were left unspoken.
If the wind never blew.
If the sun never shone.
If the birds never flew.
Would the mountains
Tumble beneath the sea?
Would the clouds
Evaporate into the canvas of blue sky?
What would you say
If I told you
These things that make life
Were what I wanted
What I need
Tell me.
What would you say
If the trees never grew
And the flowers never bloomed.
Would you tell me.

Paula O'Hare

This England

This battered land of ours;
These much visited shores.
Where good hearts and minds
Lie waiting unjust behind
Locked doors.

An army is printed on paper;
Oliver Cromwell had a dream,
Like dust it faded.
Once were bright once were strong,
Although his actions, right or wrong.

Napoleon and William the First
Besieged and enslaved us.
To those troubles we rose,
Like the phoenix, ghost ships
From the deeps,
Like the tide.

Federalism, Liberalism and Feudalism
These notions absurd!
Royalist, Patriarchal or Republican;
This is what this house is
Within these crumbling walls!

Dave Gammon